D1455798

GRAPHIC NOVELS

YOU WRITE IT!

by John Hamilton

Published by ABDO Publishing Company, 8000 West 78th Street, Suite 310, Edina, Minnesota 55439.
Copyright ©2009 by Abdo Consulting Group, Inc. International copyrights reserved in all countries.
No part of this book may be reproduced in any form without written permission from the publisher.
ABDO & Daughters™ is a trademark and logo of ABDO Publishing Company.

Printed in the United States.

Editor: Sue Hamilton
Graphic Design: Sue Hamilton
Cover Design: Neil Klinepier
Cover Illustration: Magic Wagon
Interior Photos and Illustrations: p 1 Graphic artist, iStock; p 3 Warrior art, iStock; p 4 *The Creature from the Depths*, Rod Espinosa & ABDO Publishing Group; Sketch artist, iStock; p 5 Yellow Kid, courtesy of the estate of Richard F. Outcault; Captain America comic, courtesy Joe Simon & Marvel Entertainment, *Batman: The Dark Knight Returns*, courtesy Frank Miller/Klaus Janson/Lynn Varley & DC Comics & Warner Books; p 6 *The Adventures of Tintin*, courtesy the estate of Hergé; *Bleach*, courtesy Tite Kubo & VIZ Media; p 7 *Maus I & II*, courtesy Art Spiegelman & Pantheon Books; *300*, courtesy Frank Miller/Lynn Varley & Dark Horse Books; *Watchmen*, courtesy Alan Moore/Dave Gibbons/John Higgins & DC Comics; *V For Vendetta*, courtesy Alan Moore/David Lloyd & DC Comics; p 8 *A Contract With God*, courtesy Will Eisner & DC Comics; p 9 *Sacagawea* and *The Bombing of Pearl Harbor*, Rod Espinosa & ABDO Publishing Group; p 10 Graphic artists, Comstock; p 11 Artist sketching outside, iStock; p 12 *Spider-Man* comic book & Spider-Man character, Marvel Entertainment; p 13 Index card, iStock; p 14 Good idea, iStock; p 15 Budding artist, iStock; pp 16-19 *The Legend of Sleepy Hollow*, Jeff Zornow & ABDO Publishing Group; p 20 *How To Draw Comics the Marvel Way*, courtesy Stan Lee/John Buscema & Simon & Schuster; p 21 *Silver Surfer* script, courtesy Stan Lee; Stan Lee photo, Corbis; p 23 Jack Kirby, courtesy Jack Kirby estate; *New Gods* pencils, courtesy Jack Kirby estate/Rand Hoppe & DC Comics; p 24 Wooden man & brushes, iStock; p 25 Pencil, ink, final drawing & photo of Joe Sinnott, courtesy Joe and Mark Sinnott; p 26 Man yelling, iStock; p 27 Graphic artist, AP Images; p 28 Frank Miller, AP Images; Batman & Robin, courtesy Frank Miller & DC Comics; p 29 Marjane Satrapi, AP Images, *Persepolis* cover & inside page, courtesy Marjane Satrapi & Pantheon Books.

Library of Congress Cataloging-in-Publication Data

Hamilton, John, 1959-
   You write it : graphic novel / John Hamilton.
      p. cm. -- (You write it!)
   Includes bibliographical references and index.
   ISBN 978-1-60453-505-1
   1. Graphic novels--Authorship--Juvenile literature. I. Title.

PN6710.H34 2009
741.5'6973--dc22

2008044329

Contents

SORRY, OLD GIRL. I'M USUALLY QUITE HUMANE WHEN IT COMES TO BEASTIES. HOWEVER, *YOU* MY DEAR, STAND BETWEEN *ME* AND A GREAT DEAL OF MONEY.

AAGHH!

EITHER WAY... I AM GOING TO BE VERY RICH.

What Are Graphic Novels?

A graphic novel is a long, single story told in comic-strip form. Unlike a comic book, a graphic novel's binding is usually more sturdy, like a softcover or hardcover book. Instead of being sold on newsstands, most graphic novels can be found in bookstores or special comic book stores. The history of graphic novels is relatively short, but their roots go back more than 100 years.

Newspaper comic strips became popular in the late 1800s. The first regular newspaper comic strip is usually credited to *The Yellow Kid*, which was drawn by Richard F. Outcault. Comics became wildly popular by the early 1900s, especially as color sections in Sunday newspapers. Selling comics to newspapers became a way for artistic storytellers to share their work with thousands of people.

In 1934, a man named Max Gaines had an idea: why not collect all those Sunday comic strips into a single book so people could read the cartoons without having to buy a newspaper? Gaines's idea of publishing *comic books* took off. Comic books were sold by the millions in stores and newsstands across America. Soon, artists and writers began creating stories exclusively for comic books instead of Sunday comic strips. A new industry was born.

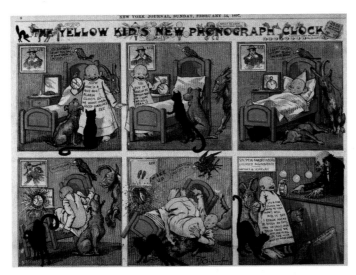

Left & Below: Richard Outcault drew the first regular newspaper comic strip, *The Yellow Kid.*

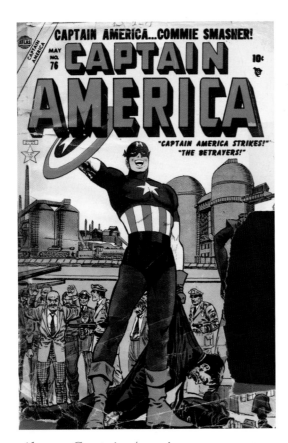

Above: Captain America was an early comic book in the 1930s. Soon, millions of comics were being created.

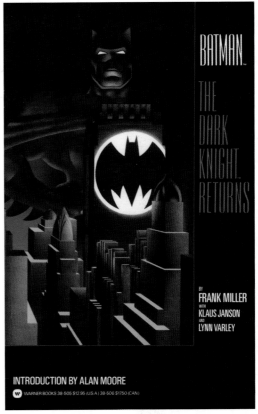

Above: Modern graphic novels, such as *Batman: The Dark Knight Returns,* are full-size books.

Above: A page from *The Adventures of Tintin.*

Above: *Bleach* is a popular Japanese graphic novel series.

In Europe, comic books with long storylines began to be published in hardcover book form. *The Adventures of Tintin*, drawn by Belgian artist Hergé, is a famous example. The series started as a long serialized comic strip reprinted into a book in 1929. Twenty-three sequels followed, the last published a few years after the author's death in 1983.

In Japan in the 1940s and 1950s, *manga* (a Japanese word for comics) started to become very popular. These stories, many of which focused on action, fantasy, and science fiction, were also collected into hardcover books. Today, manga is very popular in the United States, even by people who don't normally read American superhero-type comic books.

In the United States in the late 1970s and 1980s, publishers began collecting serialized superhero comics and republishing them as single volumes. Frank Miller's *Batman: The Dark Knight Returns* was a very successful graphic novel that was originally published as four individual comic books. *Watchmen*, by Alan Moore and Dave Gibbons, was a collected series of 12 comic books.

Maus was a graphic novel published in two parts in 1986 and 1991. It received rave reviews from critics, gaining widespread public acceptance of graphic novels as an art form. Author Art Spiegelman told the true story of his Jewish father's struggle for survival in Poland during World War II. The imaginative tale made perfect use of the graphic novel's strength in visual storytelling: Jewish people were depicted as mice, Germans were cats, and Americans were dogs. It is a moving and complex story that confronts racial prejudice, war, and the horrors of the Holocaust. *Maus* won a Pulitzer Prize in 1992.

By the turn of the 21st century, more people became interested in graphic novels. Neil Gaiman's *Sandman* books sold very well. Publishers became convinced there was a good market for graphic novels and began to produce more and more of them. Today, graphic novels about superheroes sell very well. Japanese manga continues to be very popular in the United States. Hollywood has also become interested in graphic novels. Original stories told in graphic novel form are often made into movies. Recent examples include *300*, *Watchmen*, and *V for Vendetta*.

Above: Moviemakers often turn to graphic novels for ideas. Recent examples include *300*, *Watchmen,* and *V for Vendetta.*

Who creates graphic novels? Today, they are often made by teams of people, each with their own job to fulfill, such as writers, pencilers, and inkers. However, there are many independent or low-budget graphic novels that are produced by a single person.

Creating a graphic novel is good for an artist who has a personal vision to share with the world. Visual storytelling usually takes many people to accomplish; creating a movie or stage play requires a big team. A good graphic novel can be created by one person, or even just a couple of dedicated artists. Creating a graphic novel is a way to share your vision instantly with your audience.

Graphic novels also have a reputation for dealing with difficult subjects in an honest way. Some artists examine mature themes like teen sexuality, drug abuse, or poverty. But even something simple, like the awkward years of high school, can be explored creatively and honestly within the pages of a graphic novel. One of the earliest successful graphic novels was Will Eisner's *A Contract with God*, written in 1978. It tells the story of 1930s Jewish life in New York's overcrowded and run-down tenement houses.

If you have a love of drawing and storytelling, you too can become a graphic novelist. You can get help from your friends, or maybe you want to do it yourself. Either way, producing a graphic novel is a great way to explore your creativity. You are limited only by your imagination, plus the hard work you're willing to devote to your project.

Facing Page and Above: Graphic novels are a creative way to show many kinds of topics, including religion and history.

Ideas

The number-one question asked of writers is, where do you get your ideas? It's usually asked by beginners who are afraid they don't have the imagination it takes to be successful. But as you'll soon find out, ideas are everywhere: in your head, in a book, in a movie, even in stray conversations overheard at lunch. Developing an idea into a *story* is where the hard work takes place.

How do you know if you have a good idea for a graphic novel? Like movies, graphic novels are a visual art. That is why superheroes, action/adventure, and science fiction are so popular with readers. The writer's motto "show, don't tell" is critical to a graphic novel's success.

That doesn't mean you can't explore serious subjects. In fact, graphic novels have a long history of examining topics that other media shy away from, such as teen social problems or substance abuse. But by and large, the most popular graphic novels stick to certain tried-and-true genres. These include stories about superheroes, crime, science fiction, fantasy, horror, and action/adventure.

Of course, you can easily incorporate a more personal story into one of the larger genres. Maybe a superhero is filled with rage because he was abused as a child, and must learn to deal with his tragic past. Or maybe your adventure hero also wrestles with drug or alcohol abuse. (Sherlock Holmes was a famous cocaine user.) These kinds of blended stories—issues we often face in real life combined with "larger-than-life" genre adventures—can be very powerful and entertaining at the same time.

Coming Up With Ideas

- You must *read* in order to write. Read a lot. Every day. Graphic novels are available in most bookstores, newsstands, and specialty comic stores, as well as online retailers like Amazon.com. Your school or local library might also have graphic novels available for you to check out.

- Write what you know. Use your past experiences, then translate them into ideas.

- Brainstorm. Time yourself for two minutes. Jot down any ideas that pop into your head. Don't edit yourself, even if you think the ideas are stupid. They may spark even more creativity later.

- Keep a daily journal. It can be like a diary or a blog, but it can also include ideas that pop into your head, drawings, articles, photos, etc. As you collect information, you'll see patterns begin to emerge of things that interest you the most. Explore these themes.

- Write down your dreams. And your daydreams.

Characters

What's more important, plot or character? Some writers say plot. After all, your readers are expecting a good story. On the other hand, think of the best books you've ever read. Chances are, what you remember most are the interesting characters.

The truth is, both elements are critical to good storytelling. You can't have one without the other. The reason characters are so memorable is because they are the key to unlocking the emotions of your story. You empathize with them, feel what they feel. Through great characters, you have an emotional stake in the outcome of the story. If you don't care about the characters, why should you care how the story turns out?

Character Biographies

Good writers are people watchers. Study the people you meet every day, your friends and enemies, even yourself. Start a character journal; write down what makes these people interesting to you. Observe their physical characteristics and their behavior. How do they dress? How do they walk and talk? Exaggerate any traits, quirks, or inside jokes that come to mind. Mold and twist these traits into your own fictional characters.

Backstory is the history you create for your characters. Most of it may never make it into your final draft, but it helps make your characters seem more "real" as you write. Many writers find it helpful to create very detailed biographies of all their major characters. This sometimes helps you discover your characters' strengths and weaknesses, which you can use later when you throw them into the boiling stew of your plot.

Character Biography Checklist

Below is a list of traits you might want to answer for each of your characters. You should at least know this backstory information for your hero and main villain. What other traits can you think of that will round out your characters' biographies?

Character Biography Checklist

✓ Character's full name
✓ Nickname
✓ Age/Birthdate
✓ Color of eyes/hair
✓ Height/weight
✓ Ethnic background
✓ Physical imperfections
✓ Glasses/contacts
✓ Family background
✓ Spouse/children
✓ Religion
✓ Politics
✓ School
✓ Special skills
✓ Military
✓ Job/profession
✓ Hobbies/sports
✓ Bad habits
✓ Fears
✓ Hopes and dreams

Story

Coming up with an actual plot can be a daunting task. It becomes more manageable if you break it down into smaller parts. You've probably already learned in school that fiction has three key elements: a beginning, middle, and an end, sometimes referred to as Acts I, II, and III. Acts I and III (the beginning and end) are critical pieces of the story, but are relatively short. Act II holds the guts of the story, where the majority of the action takes place.

Act I

When you begin your story, think about your characters. In a good story, strong characters are driven by their needs. These needs often conflict. How your characters resolve their conflicts is what makes the difference between a boring story and a story that's so riveting you can't put it down.

The first few pages of a graphic novel are critically important. Often called the "hook," this part of the story usually establishes the setting and major characters. Many writers, surprisingly, don't start their stories at the beginning. Instead, their stories start with a bang, right in the middle of the action, with the hero embroiled in an exciting scene. Only after the scene's action is resolved do we take a step back and reveal the major characters and setting. Remember, character is action. By starting with an action scene, we automatically learn something about the main character.

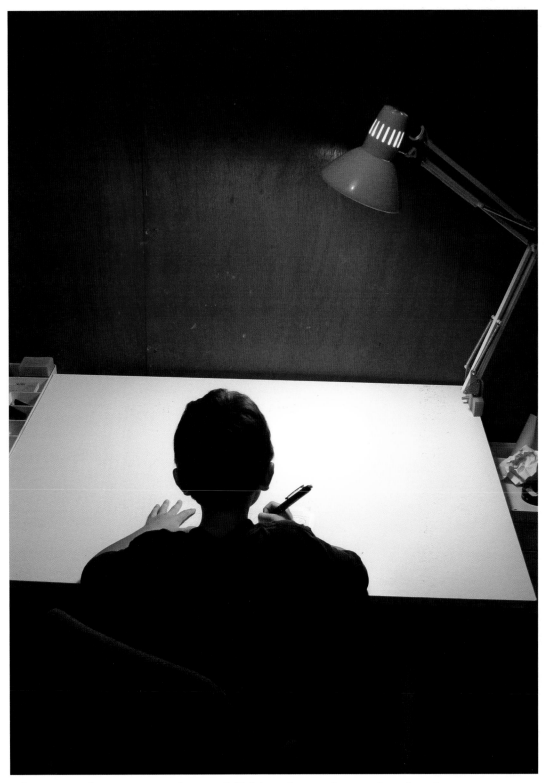

Above: Begin your story by establishing the setting and major characters.

After the beginning, how do you establish the plot and tie it all together? In *The Hero With a Thousand Faces*, author Joseph Campbell described patterns that are common to almost all works of fiction. They form a structure that authors use to tell the same basic tale, a story about a hero who goes on a quest to find a prize and bring it back to his or her tribe. This kind of story structure is very popular in fiction today.

Some writers think it's useful to keep this "hero's journey" in mind as they dream up their own stories. Of course, you don't have to rigidly follow the structure. It is merely a guide.

The beginning of the story introduces the hero before the adventure begins. Typical graphic novels show the hero in his or her "normal" world, before a creeping evil upsets the balance of all things. Time spent in the ordinary world allows the writer to identify what the hero wants, and what's at stake.

Next, a call to adventure, also called an inciting incident, happens that gets the story moving. There may be a message or temptation that calls your hero to act. The message is often delivered by a type of character, or archetype, called a herald.

Next is a point in the story called "crossing the threshold." This is where the hero makes a decision (or a decision is made for him), and he's thrown into the adventure. The hero's world is threatened, or changed, and it's up to the hero to make things right.

Right: Characters are introduced in Act I. In *The Legend of Sleepy Hollow*, readers meet the main character, the new schoolmaster, Ichabod Crane.

Setting

Setting plays a very important part in how a graphic novelist tells his or her story. If your setting is a made-up place, like in a fantasy or science fiction story, then you can draw whatever you want. On the other hand, there are advantages to having your story take place in the real world, perhaps in your own neighborhood. It may be easier for you to draw from memory. Or you can take pictures of various locations and use them for reference. Anything you need to draw is within a few miles from home. This is especially helpful for beginners. But even if you do choose a fictional setting, it sometimes adds interest to draw a real-world building or city into your fantasy world.

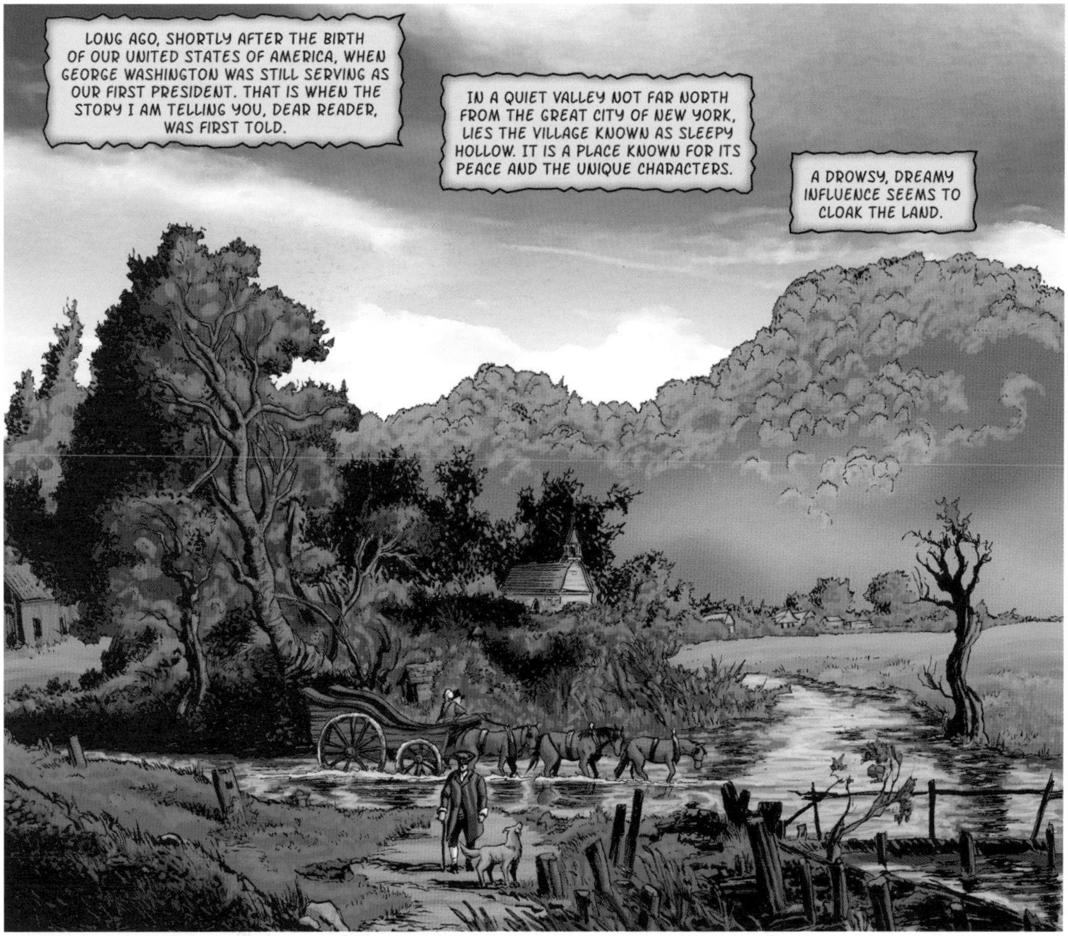
LONG AGO, SHORTLY AFTER THE BIRTH OF OUR UNITED STATES OF AMERICA, WHEN GEORGE WASHINGTON WAS STILL SERVING AS OUR FIRST PRESIDENT. THAT IS WHEN THE STORY I AM TELLING YOU, DEAR READER, WAS FIRST TOLD.
IN A QUIET VALLEY NOT FAR NORTH FROM THE GREAT CITY OF NEW YORK, LIES THE VILLAGE KNOWN AS SLEEPY HOLLOW. IT IS A PLACE KNOWN FOR ITS PEACE AND THE UNIQUE CHARACTERS.
A DROWSY, DREAMY INFLUENCE SEEMS TO CLOAK THE LAND.

Above: The setting, a peaceful place north of New York City, is established with one of the first panels in this graphic novel of *The Legend of Sleepy Hollow.*

Act II

Act II is for testing the hero. What allies does he meet? What enemies? Who is the chief villain, and what are his goals? Does our hero act alone, or does he gather a group together, a posse?

Act II is a series of rising actions and mini-climaxes. In real life, events happen in seemingly random order. But in a good story, each event the hero encounters is connected, leading to the next ordeal.

Right: The Legend of Sleepy Hollow conflict is established when readers meet the pretty Katrina and her suitor, Brom. Ichabod's easy relationship with Katrina makes Brom jealous. Brom sets out to scare Ichabod away. The question is: how far will he go to get rid of Ichabod?

Act III

This is the point in the story where the hero uses everything he's learned and faces the ultimate test. In many graphic novels, the conflict becomes a physical action; the final struggle is a fight of some kind, using a combination of skills learned during the course of the story.

It's always best if your character wins the conflict on his or her own. Beware of having another character swoop in to save the day. This kind of ending is called a *deus ex machina*, a Latin phrase that means "machine of the gods." In some ancient Greek plays, a cage with an actor portraying a god inside was lowered onto the stage, where the god would miraculously solve the hero's seemingly hopeless problems. You've probably read books or watched movies where a similar event happened—an unexpected person or situation arises and saves the day. This is what some critics refer to as a contrived ending. Don't resort to this! You've spent the whole story building up your hero with new wisdom and skills. Let him save himself. Otherwise, what's the point of telling your story?

Above: Ichabod comes "face-to-face" with the headless horseman.

Script

Writing a script for a graphic novel involves breaking your story down into pages, and then breaking the pages into panels. If you are working with an artist, this is where you describe in detail the action and dialogue that occurs in each scene.

How many pages you devote to each scene will affect the pacing of your graphic novel. You could describe an action, such as a character driving a car, in a single panel, which would speed up the pace. Or you could slow things down, showing the character driving over the course of several panels. There is no "right" or "wrong" way to do this.

Graphic novel scripts are very personal things. Unlike screenplays, there is no set way to create one. The important thing is that you clearly communicate your intentions to your artist.

The most common way a writer communicates with an artist is with a full script. A full script gives a description of each panel on every page, including any dialogue, thought balloons, or captions. Full scripts might be typed, like the *Silver Surfer* example on the following page by comic expert Stan Lee. Stories can also take the form of a layout script, where the author draws rough thumbnail sketches of each panel to give the artist a better idea of his intentions. Writers who do their own penciling and inking often first produce a layout script.

Another type of graphic novel script is called the Marvel-style script. Made popular at Marvel Comics in the 1960s, these scripts simply tell the story without breaking down individual pages or panels. The artist is free to decide where to place the panels. Some artists love this because it gives them more freedom. Others feel like they're doing the writer's job for them. You should talk to your artist before writing a Marvel-style script.

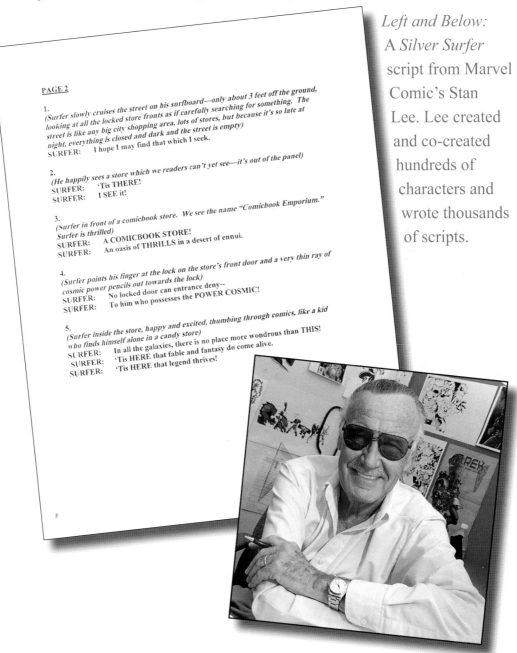

PAGE 2

1.
(Surfer slowly cruises the street on his surfboard—only about 3 feet off the ground, looking at all the locked store fronts as if carefully searching for something. The street is like any big city shopping area, lots of stores, but because it's so late at night, everything is closed and dark and the street is empty)
SURFER: I hope I may find that which I seek.

2.
(He happily sees a store which we readers can't yet see—it's out of the panel)
SURFER: 'Tis THERE!
SURFER: I SEE it!

3.
(Surfer in front of a comicbook store. We see the name "Comicbook Emporium."
Surfer is thrilled)
SURFER: A COMICBOOK STORE!
SURFER: An oasis of THRILLS in a desert of ennui.

4.
(Surfer points his finger at the lock on the store's front door and a very thin ray of cosmic power pencils out towards the lock)
SURFER: No locked door can entrance deny--
SURFER: To him who possesses the POWER COSMIC!

5.
(Surfer inside the store, happy and excited, thumbing through comics, like a kid who finds himself alone in a candy store)
SURFER: In all the galaxies, there is no place more wondrous than THIS!
SURFER: 'Tis HERE that fable and fantasy do come alive.
SURFER: 'Tis HERE that legend thrives!

Left and Below:
A *Silver Surfer* script from Marvel Comic's Stan Lee. Lee created and co-created hundreds of characters and wrote thousands of scripts.

Penciling

After the layout and script of your graphic novel are finished, it's time for the artist to begin penciling in the images for each panel. If you are doing the artwork yourself, then you already have a good idea of how the story will translate into print.

A book like this one can't teach you how to draw. There are many books, courses, and other resources available to you on the Internet. The most important thing is to practice your drawing skills every day. Also, keep in mind that you don't have to be a great artist to create an interesting graphic novel. Many crudely drawn graphic novels have received critical acclaim because of their superior storylines and creativity. Even stick figures can work if the storyline is intriguing or humorous enough to hold your reader's attention.

If you are working with an artist, he or she will draw in pencil each frame of your graphic novel. The artist decides which perspective, or "camera angle," each frame will have. Costuming, character expressions, gestures, and lighting are other important decisions made by the penciler.

The most important job of the penciler, however, is to tell the story in a definite sequence of images. A great pencil artist may come up with ideas never even dreamed of by the writer. Jack Kirby, who worked on many Marvel Comics in the 1950s, 60s, and 70s, had a legendary imagination that added to the comics' original ideas.

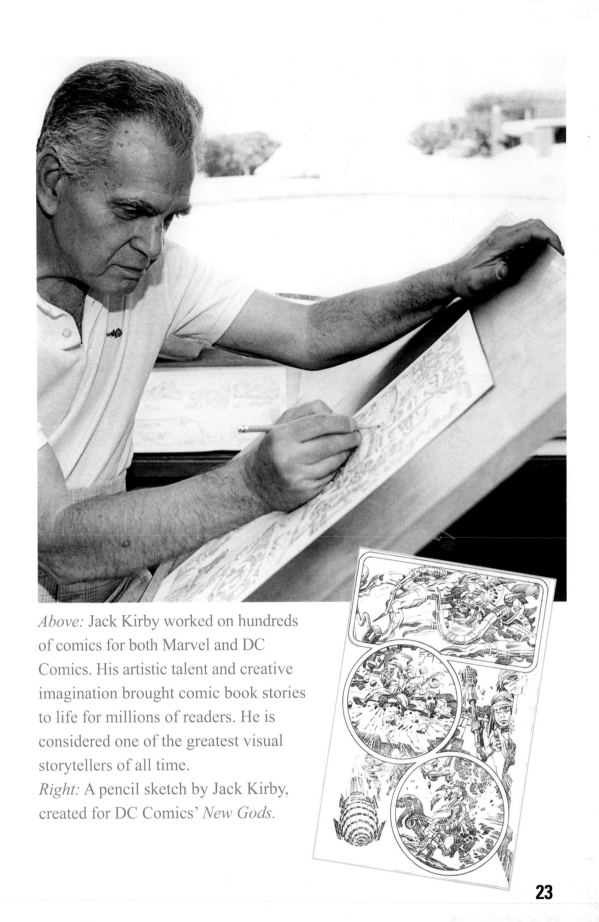

Above: Jack Kirby worked on hundreds of comics for both Marvel and DC Comics. His artistic talent and creative imagination brought comic book stories to life for millions of readers. He is considered one of the greatest visual storytellers of all time.

Right: A pencil sketch by Jack Kirby, created for DC Comics' *New Gods*.

Finishing Touches

After penciling is complete, another artist, or the one-man-band graphic novelist, applies dark ink to the sketches and then erases any remaining pencil marks. Inking is done so that the comics reproduce better when you go to press. Raw pencil sketches might be too light or smudgy in places. Inking the art gives everything a consistent look and feel, making it seem more "solid." However, an inker's job isn't just to trace over the pencil lines. Inking is a special skill that gives the artwork weight, fine detail, shading, and depth.

Another specialty skill, often applied at the same time as inking, is lettering. In the past, every graphic novel was hand lettered, which took great patience and craft. Today, graphic novels are often lettered using a computer. There are many different typefaces available, and the type is easy to output. Changes are simple. However, many artists still prefer to letter by hand. Hand lettering gives the panels a more unified look and customized feel.

Some graphic novels are printed in black-and-white, but many others have color applied. A colorist is another artist who brings creativity and craft to the job. Good coloring unifies the "look" of a graphic novel and makes it more interesting and moody. Coloring today is most often performed using a computer paint program like Adobe Photoshop.

If you are printing your own graphic novel, you may not have the budget to print in color. If you are determined to print in color, you must learn the special requirements of printing presses. Printed art has a limited number of colors that can be used. Always consult with your printer before doing the color work on your graphic novel.

Above and Left: One-man-band artist Joe Sinnott pencil-sketched, inked, and colored thousands of graphic panels for comic books, magazines, and newspapers.

Get Published

Your graphic novel is written, and all the panels are drawn, inked, and colored. Now what? Your first impulse might be to try to sell your work to major book publishers. You can either send them copies of your completed pages, or a proposal that includes your project's plot and characters, as well as some sample pages. Keep in mind that competition is very fierce. If you receive a rejection letter, don't despair. Everybody gets them! Remember, the publisher isn't rejecting *you*, only your graphic novel. Maybe your writing or artwork isn't strong enough just yet. Or maybe your graphic novel is fine, but the publisher isn't buying stories like yours at this time. Trends come and go in the marketplace, but don't try to create what you think publishers are looking for. By the time you finish your book, the fickle public will have moved on to the Next Big Thing. Simply create what you love, and the rest will follow.

If mainstream book publishing isn't for you, there are other options available. You could self publish, paying a printer to produce and bind your work into book form. This usually costs several thousand dollars, however, and seldom creates a profit for the writer and artists.

Another option is to simply photocopy your graphic novel and fold it up into book form, bound together by staples. Sell or give your graphic novel to friends or family. You can even hand-sell copies to local comic shops or comic book distributors, who might be interested in carrying graphic novels from new artists.

You can also put your work on a web site. With the right word-of-mouth advertising, you can generate a lot of traffic to your site. You might not see a lot of profit, however, since people who visit web sites like their content for free. Some people can be coaxed into giving a small amount of money if they enjoyed your work, usually through a money collection web site like Paypal.com.

Whatever form your graphic novel eventually takes, take pride in your accomplishment. You have the gift of storytelling. Sometimes you just need good timing and a little bit of luck. Just remember that the more persistent you are, the luckier you will get. Keep writing!

Above: When you're done with your first graphic novel, start on the next one. The more you practice your skills at creating a script and drawing the accompanying illustrations, the better you'll become.

SORRY, OLD GIRL. I'M USUALLY QUITE HUMANE WHEN IT COMES TO BEASTIES. HOWEVER, *YOU* MY DEAR, STAND BETWEEN *ME* AND A GREAT DEAL OF MONEY.

AAAGHH!

EITHER WAY... I AM GOING TO BE VERY RICH.

Graphic Novelist Profiles

"You can't have virtue without sin. What I'm after is having my characters' virtues defined by how they operate in a very sinful environment. That's how you test people." —Frank Miller

Frank Miller (1957-)

Frank Miller is a graphic novelist who is known for his dark and gritty style of storytelling. The worlds he creates are filled with lowlifes and criminals. Into these environments, Miller throws conflicted heroes who battle not only their adversaries, but their inner demons as well.

Miller first came onto the comics scene in the late 1970s and early 1980s. He worked for Marvel Comics on such characters as Spider-Man and John Carter: Warlord of Mars. His writing and art heavily influenced Marvel's *Daredevil* series of comic books.

In 1986, DC Comics published Miller's *Batman: The Dark Knight Returns*. First printed as a four-part series, the stories were later collected as a graphic novel. Batman's character in Miller's retelling was tough and hard-edged. The story was very popular, and heavily influenced the way future comic book heroes would be depicted.

Miller has worked on many other successful graphic novels, several of which became major motion pictures, such as *Sin City* and *300*.

Left: Graphic novelist Marjane Satrapi.
Above: The cover and a page
of Satrapi's black-and-white,
autobiographical graphic novel,
Persepolis.

"The first writing of the human being was drawing, not writing…
Image is an international language."   –Marjane Satrapi

Marjane Satrapi (1969-)

Marjane Satrapi was born in Tehran, Iran, in 1969. Her acclaimed 2001
autobiographical graphic novel, *Persepolis*, tells about her life growing up in
the 1980s during the strict Iranian Islamic Revolution. Told in simple black-
and-white images, it is a powerful yet humorous story about the costs of war
and daily life under a repressive government. It is a fascinating history of how
she and her family members survived the revolution and kept their spirits alive.

In 1983, Satrapi was sent by her parents to Vienna, Austria, to escape
the harsh regime. She later returned to Iran to go to college, studying visual
communications. Later, she moved to Paris, France, where she now works as
an artist and children's book author.

In 2007, an animated film of *Persepolis* was released, first in Europe,
then in the United States. It won a Best Animated Feature Academy Award
in 2008.

Helpful Reading

- *The Complete Idiot's Guide to Creating a Graphic Novel* by Nat Gertler and Steve Lieber

- *The Everything Guide to Writing Graphic Novels* by Mark Ellis and Melissa Martin Ellis

- *Drawing Words & Writing Pictures* by Jessica Abel & Matt Madden

- *The Writer's Journey: Mythic Structure for Writers* by Christopher Vogler

- *The Hero With a Thousand Faces* by Joseph Campbell

- *Stein on Writing* by Sol Stein

- *Self-Editing for Fiction Writers* by Renni Browne and Dave King

- *Writing Dialogue* by Tom Chiarella

- *Building Believable Characters* by Marc McCutcheon

- *Zen in the Art of Writing* by Ray Bradbury

- *The Elements of Style* by William Strunk, Jr., and E.B. White

- *The Transitive Vampire* by Karen Elizabeth Gordon

- *Roget's Super Thesaurus* by Marc McCutcheon

- *2009 Writer's Market* by Robert Brewer

- *Jeff Herman's Guide to Publishers, Editors, & Literary Agents 2009* by Jeff Herman

Glossary

Archetype — A type of character that often appears in stories. Archetypes have special functions that move the story along, such as providing the hero with needed equipment or knowledge.

Backstory — The background and history of a story's characters and setting. When writing, it is good to know as much backstory as possible, even if most of it never appears in the final manuscript.

Comic Book — A series of artistic panels that tells one or more stories, collected and bound together in book or magazine form. Starting in the 1930s, comic books were simply collections of Sunday newspaper comic strips. Later, whole comic books were devoted to single stories, or a small group of stories related to a single character. Even though they are called "comic" books, many have serious themes, or focus on action and adventure.

Genre — A type, or kind, of a work of art. In literature, a genre is distinguished by a common subject, theme, or style. Some genres include science fiction, fantasy, mystery, and horror.

Hook — The beginning of a story, used to grab a reader's interest.

Pulitzer Prize — An award for great achievement in American literature, music, or journalism.

Serialize — To publish, in regular intervals, a long story that is broken up into short chapters. Magazines and newspapers often serialized comic strips with long stories in weekly or monthly installments. Later, these comics were collected into softcover or hardcover books and sold as single graphic novels.

Index